Managing a MEDIATION PROCESS

Amy L. Smith and David R. Smock

The Peacemaker's Toolkit Series Editors: A. Heather Coyne and Nigel Quinney

United States Institute of Peace
1200 17th Street NW, Suite 200
Washington, DC 20036-3011

Phone: 202-457-1700
Fax: 202-429-6063
E-mail: usip_requests@usip.org
Web: www.usip.org

First published 2008

Printed in the United States of America

The paper used in this publication meets the minimum requirements of American National Standards for Information Science—Permance of Paper for Printed Library Materials, ANSI Z39.48-1984.

Library of Congress Cataloging-in-Publication Data

Smith, Amy L.
Managing a mediation proces / Amy L. Smith and David R. Smock.
p. cm.
ISBN 978-1-60127-037-5 (pbk. : alk. paper)
1. Pacific settlement of international disputes. 2. Mediation. 3. Conflict management. I. Smock, David R. II. Title.
JZ6010.S65 2008
303.6'9- -dc22

2008020857

Contents

Introduction

Mediation is an art form, incorporating intuition, subtlety, and vision. Yet it is also a craft with transferable tools, definable tasks, and management challenges. The purpose of *The Peacemaker's Toolkit* series is to help mediators learn from one another by distilling from their hard-won experience useful lessons about the tools of their trade, the tasks they must perform, and the challenges they must overcome. Each handbook in the series addresses a particular facet of the work of mediating violent conflicts. Individually and collectively, these books should help mediators maintain a clear sense of strategic direction as they strive to help make peace.

The Peacemaker's Toolkit is a project of the United States Institute of Peace (USIP), which for twenty-five years has supported the work of mediators through research, training, workshops, and publications designed to discover and disseminate the keys to effective mediation. The Institute—mandated by the U.S. Congress to help prevent, manage, and resolve international conflict through nonviolent means—has conceived of *The Peacemaker's Toolkit* as a way of combining its own accumulated expertise with that of other organizations active in the field of mediation. Most publications in the series are produced jointly by the Institute and a partner organization. All publications are carefully reviewed before publication by highly experienced mediators to ensure that the final product will be a useful and reliable resource for practitioners.

This handbook, the first in *The Peacemaker's Toolkit* series, offers an overview of the process of mediating interstate and intrastate conflicts. Each of its six chapters covers a different step in the process, identifying what needs to be done at that step and how best to accomplish it. The steps are numbered and reflect the order in which various tasks are often begun. It is important to note, however, that once begun, some steps may be ongoing, overlapping with and outlasting other, later steps. For example, conflict assessment, which launches the entire mediation process, will likely continue in some fashion throughout the process until a peace agreement is reached. The other five steps focus, in turn, on ensuring mediator readiness, determining and enhancing ripeness, managing negotiations between the parties to the conflict, encouraging and coordinating with Track-II endeavors, and constructing and implementing an agreement.

Managing a Mediation Process, it should be noted, views mediation from the perspective of a mediator involved in an official, or "Track-I," effort. Most steps of the process, however, would also apply to unofficial, "Track-II," efforts. Other books in *The Peacemaker's Toolkit* series will focus on Track-II efforts and explore in depth the relationship between Tracks I and II.

Consolidating the practical wisdom of managing a mediation process into an easily digestible format, *Managing a Mediation Process* is designed to help mediators identify areas where they may need more research or preparation, as well as options and strategies relevant to the particular case on which they are working. Examples *(in italics in the text)* from past mediation efforts are provided to illustrate how various strategies have played out in practice and how various factors have facilitated or impeded the mediator's work. Whether used by a practitioner to initiate detailed planning or reviewed at the last minute on the flight to the negotiations, this handbook, like others in *The Peacemaker's Toolkit* series, is intended to be a practical and valuable resource for mediators.

Further Reading

A handbook of this brevity can provide only a rough guide to a subject as intricate and multifaceted as mediation, and readers should consult other, more detailed studies to amplify and refine the ideas and advice given in the following chapters. An excellent place to start further research is with three volumes—all published by the United States Institute of Peace and all either edited or authored by the trio of Chester A. Crocker, Fen Osler Hampson, and Pamela Aall—that have formed the basis for much of the discussion in this book: *Grasping the Nettle: Analyzing Cases of Intractable Conflict* (2005); *Taming Intractable Conflicts: Mediation in the Hardest Cases* (2004); and *Herding Cats: Multiparty Mediation in a Complex World* (1999). This book also reflects the core writings of I. William Zartman on the concept of ripeness and draws on the collected resources of BeyondIntractability.org, an online knowledge base for conflict management.

The Online Version

There is an online version of *The Peacemaker's Toolkit* that includes not only the text of this handbook but also connects readers to a vast web of information. Links in the online version give readers immediate access to a considerable variety of publications, news reports, directories, and other sources of data regarding ongoing mediation initiatives, case studies, theoretical frameworks, and education and training. These links enable the online *Toolkit* to serve as a "you are here" map to the larger literature on mediation. The online version is available at www.usip.org/mediation/peacemaker_toolkit.html.

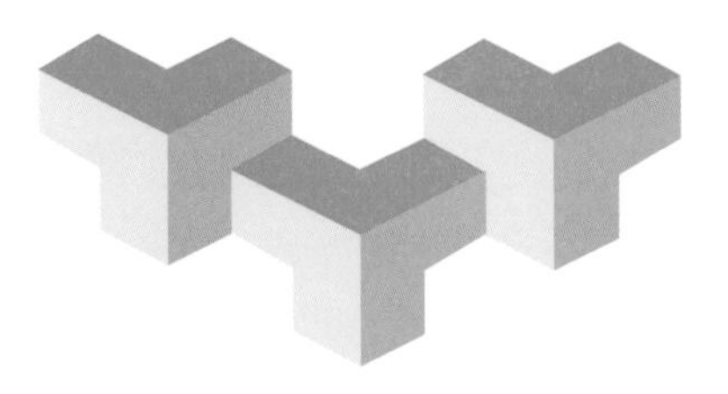

STEP ONE

Assess the Conflict

The first step in any mediation effort should be to assess the conflict. That assessment should neither overwhelm the mediator with extraneous information from an exhaustive historical review, nor be so cursory as to risk generating only foregone conclusions and standard formulas. Instead, conflict analysis should provide a contextualized understanding of the conflict and answer questions of strategy: at what level to engage, how to gain leverage, and on whom to focus efforts.

That said, the mediator frequently works in muddy waters in regard to the knowledge at his or her disposal; required information may be ambiguous, flawed, or unavailable. The mediator may often have to navigate relying not on hard information but on experience, intuition, and common sense, but it helps to know what questions the mediator would ideally like answered.

Generally, this step involves four activities: (1) understanding what the conflict is about, (2) understanding who the actors are, (3) understanding the larger context, and (4) understanding sources of power and leverage.

Understand What the Conflict Is About

The basic question, "What is this conflict about?" can be conceptualized in a number of ways. Some analysts use conflict analysis tools that focus on issues and interests; others on grievances, needs, and relationships; while others create problem trees or possibility trees. Each of these approaches has value, but ultimately the most valuable tools are simply those that the mediator finds most useful.

Analyze the History and Causes of the Conflict

In order to communicate effectively with parties, a mediator needs to grasp the history and content of the conflict as it matters to the participants, including key symbols and turning points. Some of this will be ancient history; some of it will be fabricated.

> **➢ Identify what is being contested.**
>
> **➢ Trace the trajectory of core and emerging issues.**

What is being contested? Is it territory, sovereignty and local autonomy, control of natural resources or wealth, religious or ethnic identity? What are the commonalities among the different issues? A conflict may have multiple manifestations, being "about" different things at different levels: local, national, regional, and international. For example, a local or even a private land dispute may become an ethnic dispute over land access at the community or municipal level, attracting other partisan issues at the national level.

To the uninformed, the conflict between North and South Sudan may appear to be a case of Muslim versus Christian, when in fact the sources of conflict are much more complex.

The extended trajectory of a conflict may also include a shifting range of core issues, with a new area of contestation arising whenever another is resolved. The mediator should trace this trajectory to fully understand the history and causes of the conflict.

Assess Positions and Interests

> **➢ Identify issues and positions.**
>
> **➢ Differentiate between stated positions and underlying interests.**
>
> **➢ Consider interaction among issues, positions, and interests.**

The mediator must identify the positions of the parties to the conflict and the issues that divide them. Their perceptions and misperceptions of themselves and their antagonists, of the course of the conflict thus far, and of the process of negotiation will be central to their willingness to engage in mediation. What factors, including personal and cultural ones, underlie positions? For example, does a leader fear that he or she may be killed if peace becomes a reality, or does the society regard compromise as a sign of weakness?

The mediator should differentiate between the stated positions and the underlying interests of the key actors. How will different conflict resolution scenarios affect underlying interests? Even if issues being contested are settled, actors' interests might continue to drive the conflict. Who has an interest in keeping the conflict going? For some people, for instance, the conflict may be a source of power or wealth or a means of avoiding justice. Some of these interests may be legitimate and could be satisfied by means other than conflict.

How do the issues, positions, and interests of the antagonists line up? For example, do the rebels really want secession, or are their demands an expression of a need for greater security? Perhaps they do indeed need more security, but perhaps their claims of insecurity are just part of a strategy to gain control of the state.

Understand the Actors

Ultimately, the local society must be responsible for the resolution of conflict, but it is likely that a number of other actors will be involved. Effective mediators devise different forms of engagement for different actors. Some actors will have a place at the table. Others will have observer status. Private and public consultations will occur in many different forms. Part of an effective mediation strategy is finding constructive forms of inclusion for different actors.

Analyze the Parties to the Conflict

The mediator should examine the groups directly involved in the conflict, including how they define themselves and whether they possess political as well as military wings. What are the groups' profiles within the larger society? How large a part of the overall population do they represent? What is the quality of their connection to their constituency?

The group's internal organizational structure is an important consideration. What is the hierarchy or chain of command? Is the chain of command generally stable and effective? The concentration of power within the group should be taken into account, including how decisions are made and who participates in decision

- **Examine the groups involved.**
- **Analyze their internal structure.**
- **Identify leaders and bases of authority.**
- **Ascertain support for spoilers.**
- **Assess skills, resources, and influence of leadership.**

making, as well as the cohesiveness of the group and any existing or potential internal factions.

The failure of the Darfur Peace Agreement in 2006 derived in part from a failure of the mediators to recognize the complexity of the factionalism within the rebel movements. Peace negotiations in Burundi have also been complicated by multiple rebel movements and factions, with varying levels of commitment to the peace process.

The mediator should identify the top leaders and the basis of their authority (e.g., military prowess, political skill, popular following, or potential to lead after the conflict). How are the leaders accountable to their group and to the populace? How removed are they from the costs and consequences of the conflict? It is helpful to consider the consequences for the conflict of a change in the top leadership.

Midlevel leaders may be significant to a negotiation. In profiling the middle level, the mediator should determine how independent its members are from the top leadership and identify the relevant social networks to which they may be connected (e.g., the business community, professional associations, churches, academic institutions, and the arts community).

Spoilers may attempt to scuttle a peace process. The mediator should try to determine their interests for doing so, the support they might command, and the channels they might use to obtain resources to continue the conflict.

Parties need leadership skills and organizational forms that can serve peaceful as well as military functions. Parties will also require resources to conduct a negotiation effectively and the capacity not only to reach decisions but also to deliver their constituencies. The mediator should assess the relevant skills, resources, and influence of the different parties.

Recognizing weaknesses in the Palestine Liberation Organization's negotiating capability, the United Kingdom supported the development of a new Negotiation Support Unit to enhance the skills of the Palestinian team in its negotiations with Israelis and various international mediators.

A mediator generally does not have the power to select the negotiating counterparts in a peace process. Being fully informed about the parties to the conflict will help a mediator devise a strategy appropriate for moving those parties toward peace.

Analyze Civil Society and the Populace

The mediator should assess the organization of civil society, including patterns of civic engagement and representation. What civic organizations or associations continue to operate (e.g., political parties, professional organizations, labor unions, village councils, religious institutions, social clubs)? Some of these may be capable of bringing pressure to bear on militant groups. Some may have cross-cutting memberships and could initiate or house early, low-profile contact between parties. Some may possess relevant skills for negotiating or administering portions of a peace agreement. Some might evolve into political parties and offer a workable alternative to combatant-based political parties.

> ➤ **Assess the organization of civil society.**
>
> ➤ **Determine the involvement of the populace in the conflict.**
>
> ➤ **Understand the living conditions of the populace.**

How directly involved is the populace in the conflict? Is civil society represented by the parties directly engaged in the conflict? Does it actively support the parties to the conflict? The means available to civil society for effectively holding conflict leaders accountable should be taken into consideration.

In order to construct a peace agreement that can be successfully implemented, it is essential to understand the basic condition of the populace. The mediator should assess the populace's existing level of security and how the populace fits into existing governance, legal, economic, and social structures. The mediator should also learn about the capacity of the society to maintain communal structures, the availability of humanitarian aid, and the extent of geographic dispersal. Other issues to bear in mind are the numbers of and provisions for refugees and internally displaced persons.

Societal participation in a peace process can include many different activities and degrees of engagement. Some individuals or groups may play an active role, representing civil society in negotiations. Others may provide support to the process. Feasible forms of participation will be determined in part by the preexisting profile and organizational assets of civil society.

Identify International Actors

Other states (especially neighboring or powerful states with close relations with the parties), as well as regional or international organizations may influence local parties. Are there interested states that could thwart or assist the mediation effort? What leverage do they bring to the table? Who will behave as an ally to or adversary of the conflict parties?

- **Identify potentially influential states and international organizations.**
- **Assess their leverage.**

Differences between Russia and the Western powers over the peace agreement for Kosovo created obstacles to its adoption and implementation.

States that are able and willing to serve as guarantors of a peace settlement should be identified. What sources of support can they bring to make a settlement more attractive and help with its implementation?

The roles that international and regional organizations are playing or could play in the peace process should also be considered. What is the degree of international public attention to the conflict? Wider international or regional interest may also have a significant impact on prospects for peace.

Identify Other Players

Actors such as diasporas, non-governmental organizations (NGOs), and media can derail a peace process or help to keep it on track. They may not be central participants in a negotiation, but no mediation strategy should neglect them.

- **Profile diasporas.**
- **Assess the involvement of NGOs.**
- **Identify relevant media and their roles.**

Diasporas. Diasporas can have a large impact on peace processes. The mediator should create a clear profile of the diaspora or diasporas involved in the conflict, including their size, concentration, and connection to the country of origin. A diaspora may include a shadow government or people interested in becoming post-conflict leaders who have maintained links to constituencies. It may send resources (money, arms, or even combatants) to the conflict. Perhaps it could bring pressure on the government where it is located to either support or obstruct a peace process.

The Liberian diaspora has played a positive role in supporting post-conflict development.

International Non-Governmental Organizations. Determine if international NGOs are providing humanitarian aid or engaged in other projects locally. If so, the mediator should determine the length of their involvement and their possession of local ties, staff, and language skills. Are they a trusted local presence? If they are involved with communities on both sides of the conflict, they could play a valuable role in a peace process.

Media. The mediator must acquire a keen understanding of local media, including mass media, the media by which the elite communicate with one another, and any forms of popular alternative or independent media. Who controls the media? How do they do so (e.g., by financing, regulation, or technology)? Have the local media played a direct role in the conflict (e.g., by stoking intercommunal hatred and inciting violence)? The mediator should assess the quality of the media coverage both of the conflict and of peace efforts.

Understand the Larger Context

Peace settlements may well include transformative elements that, over time, will radically change a society. But the achievement of those transformations requires a settlement that is compatible with the society's evolving institutional profile and with the regional context.

Identify Indigenous and International Institutions for Managing Conflict

The mediator should take into account institutions and processes that the society already possesses for dealing with conflict nonviolently. Some peace processes will be able to take advantage of these, while others will have to engineer substantially new bodies and systems.

- **Assess existing government, legal, economic, social, and security institutions and processes.**
- **Assess existing and potential international institutions and processes.**

The mediator should consider the political history of the country in conflict, including the stability, effectiveness, and legitimacy of its governing institutions. How has the country handled political contention? Is there space for dissent or a tradition of a loyal opposition? Will existing legal, economic, social, and security institutions be capable of accommodating and sustaining the changes required by a settlement, such as absorbing former combatants or implementing reconciliation programs?

Through economic incentives and political accommodation, Mozambique managed to demobilize and absorb RENAMO rebels in the 1990s.

In the international context, it is imperative to assess existing and potential international institutions and processes for managing conflicts such as criminal tribunals, "contact" and "friends" groups, and relevant international conflict resolution mechanisms.

Identify and Address Characteristics of Intractability

International mediation is often a last resort for the parties to a conflict, and thus when a mediator finally comes onto the scene, he or she faces a very stubborn and challenging situation. Many factors can make a conflict protracted or unusually difficult to resolve: for instance, cocooned elites, the absence of real pressure for a settlement, fear of accountability, identity politics, material stakes, outside manipulation, the lack of outside help or wider security mechanisms, and the impact of previous, failed attempts at mediation.

Thorough strategic assessment of the conflict is even more critical in these protracted cases in order to identify points of leverage that may encourage the parties to see the costs of continued fighting in a different way and to entertain options other than violence. The mediation strategy should address the characteristics of intractability as well as the root causes of the conflict.

Failure to recognize that Jonas Savimbi was not prepared to cooperate in the implementation of any peace agreement for Angola unless it made him head of state led to the unraveling of the Bicesse Peace Accord and the Lusaka Accords.

Understand Sources of Power and Leverage

Identify Material Resources and Parties' Control over Them

Antagonists may depend on many forms of power: for instance, control of armed forces and materiel, territorial control, control of natural resources or wealth, popular support and legitimacy, external diplomatic or political support. The mediator should pay particular attention to antagonists' key sources of material resources, including state assets, commodity exports, predation on local populations, theft of humanitarian aid, and diaspora funding. Is the antagonists' hold on these resources secure and sustainable?

One reason why the Colombian government is more likely to reach a peace agreement with ELN than with FARC is that ELN does not have the economic base in drug trafficking that FARC has.

Significant nonmaterial resources of the different parties, such as popular support, fear (of power holders or of opponents), community cohesion, control of media, and endorsement by spiritual leaders should also be factored into the mediator's calculations.

Interrupting or protecting a flow of resources might give the mediator strategic leverage. The mediator should explore helping parties gain and secure access to resources by means other than violent conflict and should determine what forms of resource-sharing are feasible. The mediator should also identify what resources currently deployed for conflict might be turned toward peacemaking.

Assess the Relative Strength of Parties and How It Is Changing

Which, if any, of the antagonists has the upper hand in the conflict? Is this situation stable or dynamic? Ample staying power and self-sufficiency may make a party less susceptible to pressure. Parties may also be well informed or misinformed about their relative strength. Would different information alter interpretations of the balance of power? Understanding the balance of power between parties may help elites recognize a stalemate and thus hasten the ripeness of a conflict for resolution.

Sources of Leverage

- Support of other states or groups of states, especially those that can help to neutralize potential opponents of the mediation.
- The balance of forces in the conflict itself, a form of influence that the mediator effectively draws from a stalemate in order to persuade recalcitrant parties that there is no military or unilateral solution.
- The mediator's bilateral relationships with the parties, bearing in mind at all times the necessity of keeping both parties under pressure to move toward settlement.
- The mediator's ability to influence the parties' costs and benefits, as well as their fears and insecurities. This type of leverage comes from reassurances, external guarantees, intelligence sharing, commitments to see the settlement through to full implementation, and a readiness to mobilize international resources for the dangerous transition to peace.
- The mediator's capacity to place a continuing series of hard questions and tough choices before the parties so that they are obliged to provide answers to the mediator.
- A proposed settlement formula or package. Such leverage is typically based on selling ideas to one side that—if accepted conditionally—offer the basis for obtaining movement from the other.
- Donors and other third parties that are prepared to help underwrite the costs of achieving a negotiated settlement and ensure that levels of humanitarian, social, economic, and development assistance are sufficient to effect change once a negotiated process is under way and a negotiated settlement is within sight.

Source: Adapted from Chester A. Crocker, Fen Osler Hampson, and Pamela Aall, *Taming Intractable Conflicts: Mediation in the Hardest Cases* (Washington, D.C.: United States Institute of Peace Press, 2004), 94–95.

Begin to Develop Realistic Goals

Although it is impossible to know at the beginning of a mediation process what the final outcome will be, it is essential to formulate some hypotheses about what might be achievable. In this process it is important to develop a manageable agenda and to set attainable goals. For example, a mediation process focused on the Middle East should not seek to solve all the divisive issues plaguing the region. The mediation process does need to resolve those issues that are essential to sustainable peace, but to go beyond those core issues would be to wade into a morass and endanger the success of the mediation effort.

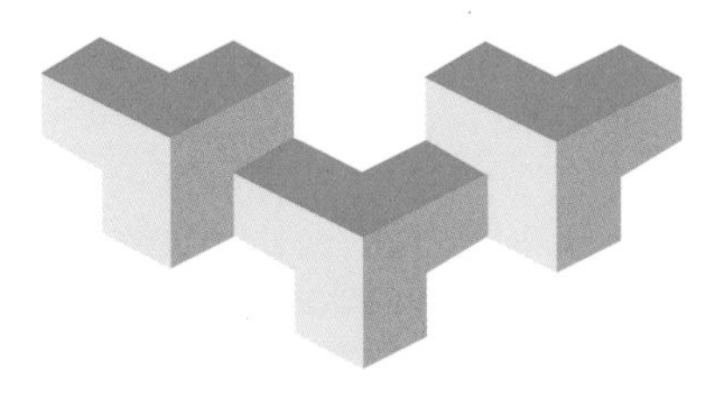

STEP TWO

Ensure Mediator Readiness

The mediator needs to know not only what needs to be done but also whether he or she is the right person to do it—whether he or she has the right skills, the right resources, and the right support to be successful. To answer these questions, mediators need to take a long, hard look at themselves and their situation. Whatever happens, a prospective mediator must not let institutional vanity or personal commitment cloud his or her judgment—the mediator, and the victims of the conflict, will pay a heavy price later for failing to acknowledge any shortcomings he or she may have to mediate a particular conflict. By the same token, however, if the mediator's self-assessment shows that he or she can make a real contribution, then the mediator should have faith in that assessment and act accordingly.

Determine What Role Is Appropriate

Determine the Right Mediation Role Given Backing and Resources

Mediators can play very diverse roles. That diversity extends far beyond the division between Track-I initiatives conducted by governments and intergovernmental organizations and Track-II endeavors launched by private organizations and individuals. Some mediators, for example, facilitate while others manipulate; some exert their political authority and flex their institutional muscle while others exploit their own weakness.

Some mediators have a high profile and the full backing of a major power or international organization. They engage official representatives of conflicting parties and may have considerable resources at their disposal. Others will have a much lower public profile but may nonetheless function with important political support and significant resources. By contrast, so-called weak mediators such as non-governmental or religious organizations have little political power of their own. That weakness, however, is a strength in that it gives them great flexibility. Unencumbered by a perceived political interest or official protocol, weak mediators can conduct their activities with greater operational dexterity than governmental mediators enjoy and can more easily gain the confidence of opposing sides.

These contrasting roles are illustrated by the "weak mediation" of the Centre for Humanitarian Dialogue and that of internationally supported Martti Ahtisaari in the Aceh peace negotiations.

Ensure That the Mediation Strategy Is Appropriate to the Mediator's Identity

A mediator's strategy must be appropriate to his or her identity. Weak negotiators cannot throw their weight around. Neither can a superpower slip in a side door or whisper over someone's shoulder. Each type of mediator has specific assets, and those are the ones he or she should deploy.

Enhance the Ability to Engage Effectively

What makes a good mediator? There are as many answers as there are good mediators. But all mediators need credibility, a portfolio of skills, and cross-cultural awareness.

Build Credibility

Credibility and trust are essential to conflict mediation. No mediator arrives with these entirely in place. Rather, credibility and trust are built over time in relationships with the different parties to the conflict.

Standards of conduct that can help a mediator earn and maintain trust include performing competently, consistently, and predictably; communicating accurately and openly with a balance between transparency and confidentiality; interacting appropriately and with equal levels of proximity with all parties; and exhibiting empathy toward and commitment to the possibility of a solution.

In any conflict, some level of distrust may remain and even be helpful. Besides encouraging reasonable vigilance about the possibilities of being manipulated or misled, distrust can usefully disrupt excessive group cohesion that might result in "groupthink" and a refusal to countenance new ideas. Distrust can be managed through shared recording practices, reporting back to the parties about what has been discussed or decided, and agreed-upon methods of monitoring and verifying actions that the parties have committed to take.

Develop and Strengthen a Broad Portfolio of Skills

Numerous studies, training manuals, workshops, and reference books provide advice on how to negotiate or to mediate a negotiation. Even an experienced mediator can benefit from these resources, which cover a wide range of topics, including the following:

- active listening, which reassures parties that their concerns have been heard and understood
- conducting open-ended questioning to encourage meaningful answers
- reframing proposals by paraphrasing and summarizing them
- describing a problem, including its symptoms and causes, before proposing solutions, and then gathering all proposals before beginning to evaluate them
- envisioning "possibility trees"—diagrams that chart the possible evolution of systems from their present condition—and identifying steps necessary to achieve imagined futures
- disaggregating and sequencing to promote movement: dividing issues into several parts, mandating or delegating preliminary work to study groups, layering discussions, or sequencing decisions
- using matched conditional statements ("yes, if") to define elements of a settlement

As might be expected, given the abundance of literature on the subject, there is no consensus on what techniques work best in which situations—but this is just as well, for the field of mediation benefits from the variety of ideas on offer. There is, however, a growing consensus about the need to complement experience, insight, and intuition with formal skills and training, and to do so before undertaking a mediation.

Recognize Cultural Differences

Different cultures communicate and negotiate differently. Cultural patterns are not homogeneous across any grouping such as nation or ethnicity, and although they exhibit considerable continuity, they are subject to change and adaptation. Nonetheless, culturally distinctive styles and expectations regarding expression and interpretation are deeply relevant to a process of mediation. Mediators should not only be able to speak and read the local language (or have reliable interpreters who can) but should also be familiar with the local cultural styles of communication: for instance, forms of courtesy; uses of humor; patterns of reciprocity; and ways of conveying respect, gratitude, or disapproval and of declining an offer or expressing criticism. Cross-cultural preparation will make communication more effective and help the mediator avoid unintentional damage.

- **Become familiar with local styles of communication.**
- **Consider how the mediator's identity will be received.**

During the transition from apartheid in South Africa in 1994, Henry Kissinger and Lord Peter Carrington were unable to successfully mediate an end to the crisis between the ANC and Inkatha. But another member of the mission, Professor Washington Okumu from Kenya, in part through his greater understanding of the involved cultures, was able to bring the two sides to agreement.

Another cross-cultural aspect of mediation is the perception by the parties of the mediator's cultural identity. Some aspects of the mediator's identity (notably, nationality, ethnicity, religion, and gender) impact the mediation. A mediator should give some thought to how this might affect an intervention. The mediation team should be designed with an eye to cross-cultural perceptions, as well as with regard for the skill, experience, and acumen of prospective team members. For example, the inclusion of women among top mediators might encourage the parties to the conflict to put some women on their own negotiating teams, thereby increasing the chances that women's interests and issues will appear on the negotiating agenda.

Ensure Adequate Authority and Resources

Obtain a Clear Mandate

In order to generate appropriate strategies, mediation initiatives need clear mandates. The underlying purpose of the mandate may be to resolve a conflict, to contain it so as to maintain regional stability, or to freeze it until anticipated contextual changes occur. Sometimes, the goal of a mediation is merely to create political cover; a state may send an envoy to a conflict zone so as to be seen to be doing something, but the conflict may actually receive little attention. Strategies that exceed mandates are unlikely to find political support.

Build and Sustain Political Support

To pursue a peace process with confidence and credibility, mediators need consistent political support. Predictable rhythms such as the term of office for an organization's leadership or the election cycle of the sponsoring nation will affect support for mediation. A mediator should be attentive to other major events that will affect the sponsor's political support. Domestic lobbies or international players may bring pressure regarding the conflict. Will the government or organization be willing and able to deflect such pressure, insulating the mediation initiative? Might the mediator use such pressure to influence the outcome of the peace process?

Obtain the Necessary Resources and Staying Power

The institutional sponsor of a mediation should provide decision-making authority, open channels of communication with the parties and other stakeholders, expertise for specific tasks, and counsel. It should also provide or pay for the full range of logistics and for adequate staff and administrative support.

- **Obtain a clear mandate.**
- **Ensure sponsor provides adequate resources and support.**
- **Plan and budget for the long run.**

Both institutional support and material resources are needed throughout the entire mediation effort. Peace processes are typically protracted, going through many phases and rotations of staff. Those that are truncated, under-resourced, or abandoned prematurely can do grave damage, exacerbating the intractability of a conflict.

The individual effort of Betty Bigombe, a former Ugandan cabinet minister, to mediate between the Ugandan government and the Lord's Resistance Army was badly hampered by the lack of institutional support for her private initiative.

Making Use of the Mediator's Emotions

Mediators must not neglect their own material and emotional needs during the course of what is typically a demanding and strenuous process. Mediators are likely to feel frustration and even anger with the parties or the process, and in some cases may even feel that they are in physical danger. These sentiments can impact the mediator's performance and interaction with the parties. The mediator should recognize these emotions and take steps either to mitigate them or to channel them in support of the process. A controlled loss of temper by the mediator, for instance, may convince parties of the seriousness not only of the mediator's resolve but also of their own situation. Similarly, a mediator who insists on and receives adequate personal security is more likely not only to reach out to some armed groups but also to confront them with information and ideas they would prefer not to hear.

Know When Not to Mediate

Ignoring protracted conflicts (on such grounds as they are containable, too complex, a low strategic priority, someone else's problem, or the subject of previous intervention failures) risks both intractability and contagion. Nonetheless, valid reasons do exist for deciding not to launch a mediation initiation or to withdraw from an ongoing effort.

Avoid Mediation if the Sponsor Lacks Commitment, Resources, or Credibility

If the sponsoring organization or government lacks either the commitment or the resources to truly support a mediation, the effort could be counterproductive. Mediators cannot work with credibility and confidence if political change in their sponsoring institution may undercut the work, if their communications will be ignored, if required decisions will be postponed, or if necessary funding will not be forthcoming. Under such conditions, the chance that mediation will fail increases, and the risk of failure is not only that this effort is wasted but that it may deepen the intractability of the conflict by increasing suspicion and cynicism among the parties to the conflict and antipathy toward future mediators.

Another circumstance in which mediation may be inappropriate is when the prospective mediator or sponsoring organization is too closely aligned with one party or too directly involved in the conflict to be balanced and/or credible. This is not to say that a mediator must be impartial to be effective, but a mediator does need to be capable politically of pressing and influencing both sides toward a settlement.

In the 1980s, Chester Crocker, U.S. assistant secretary of state for African affairs, effectively mediated between Cuba, Angola, and South Africa for the removal of Cuban troops from Angola despite U.S. enmity toward the Cuban government.

Assured success is not a requirement for beginning a mediation; the odds of making a constructive impact are much higher in a mediation that commands political and financial support and standing.

Avoid Mediation if the Conflict Is Not Ripe for Resolution

Mediation may not be the right answer when the parties do not demonstrate serious intention to explore a political solution. In such circumstances, the mediator needs to test parties' motives and avoid pleading for the engagement. The mediator should be cautious about engaging when mediation may play into the hands of a dominant party, legitimizing actions by the parties that may cross the line of acceptable conduct.

- **Avoid mediation if parties lack the intent to settle.**
- **Consider alternative means of engagement.**

The best response in some conflict situations, in other words, may be benign neglect, coercive diplomacy, or even threatening the use of force rather than mediation. There may also be times when the would-be mediator is best advised to undertake activities aimed at ripening the conflict.

The subjects of assessing and enhancing ripeness are explored in the next chapter.

Know When to Withdraw

Ongoing mediation initiatives should be regularly evaluated. In some situations, a lack of clear progress is best met with renewed commitment and the introduction of new forms of leverage or new settlement formulas; in other settings, the best option might be to focus on protecting the peace process itself until more propitious conditions emerge. In some contexts, however, withdrawal may be the most responsible action. This is the case if the process is clearly being pursued in bad faith by one or more parties (such as using a cease-fire to rebuild fighting capacity) or if it is heading to a settlement that the mediator judges to be unworkable, illegal, or unethical.

- **Consider withdrawal if settlement would be undesirable.**
- **Consider withdrawal if it is impossible to operate equitably.**
- **Evaluate reasons for withdrawal to inform future efforts.**

Former U.S. secretary of state James Baker terminated his efforts as mediator in the Western Sahara because of the parties' lack of willingness to compromise and the inability of the UN Security Council to unify behind the mediation effort.

A mediator might also withdraw if it becomes impossible for him or her to operate equitably or to ensure that the conduct of negotiations is meeting minimal standards of security or fairness.

Withdrawing from a peace process presents its own challenges. By staying in an unproductive process, a mediator risks providing cover for those using the talks to stall or distort the process. By departing, a mediator risks being made a scapegoat for the failure of talks. Part of managing the situation will include evaluating the mediation, identifying reasons for the failure, and assessing what parts of the mediation might be salvaged in a later iteration, perhaps conducted by a different type of mediator with a different approach or different resources.

The termination of a mediation process does not necessarily mean failure. One mediation process often builds on previous efforts. An effort that does not directly lead to peace may nevertheless contribute to the success of a subsequent process.

Although the Aceh mediation managed by the Centre for Humanitarian Dialogue, a Swiss NGO, did not result in a sustained peace, it provided a platform upon which the next and successful mediation process of Martti Ahtisaari was built.

A mediation process that keeps the conflict from deteriorating further, even if it does not result in sustained peace, constitutes a positive contribution.

Manage Multiple Mediators

Assess Roles Played by Other Mediators

While some conflicts are ignored, others attract a plethora of mediators. A multiplicity of mediators can sometimes be helpful. New actors can enliven stalled talks or open new avenues of communication. Mediators with specific skills or expertise can handle particular facets of negotiations. Working in cooperation, multiple mediators can isolate spoilers, increase leverage, distribute burdens, divide tasks, create momentum, and provide credible guarantees.

But a crowded field also causes problems. If mediators do not have a shared understanding of the problem, they may work at cross-purposes. This generates mixed messages about which negotiation initiative the international community is backing. A multiplicity of mediators also encourages forum shopping, as parties seek to work with mediators perceived to favor their side, and allows parties to play mediators against each other.

A plethora of workshops and meetings can create meeting overload and communications gridlock, wasting finite resources and taxing the leadership involved in numerous initiatives. The process can become unfocused and unwieldy.

Ahmedou Ould-Abdullah resigned as the UN secretary-general's special representative to Burundi in 1995 because of the confusion created by the multiplicity of international negotiators, envoys, and mediators.

If mediators are seen to compete or criticize each other, this can undercut the practice of mediation. Finally, when efforts fail, a multiplicity of mediators in the field can mean that responsibility is diluted, with none taking on the task of analyzing what went wrong.

Communicate, Coordinate, and Cooperate with Other Mediators

An environment with multiple mediators calls for careful communication, coordination, and cooperation to ensure a coherent and unified mediation effort. Ideally, cooperation will involve a conscious division of labor and perhaps even sequenced interventions that build on the strengths of different actors and encourage interdependence. Even in loosely coordinated endeavors, mediators should keep one another informed and refrain from public criticism of parallel efforts. (The subject of coordination between Track-I and Track-II mediators is explored in more detail in a later chapter.)

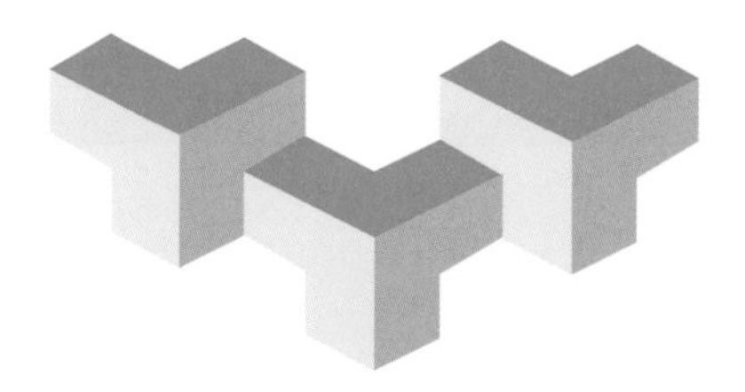

STEP THREE

Ensure Conflict Ripeness

In addition to ensuring that he or she is ready to tackle a conflict, the mediator should also ensure that the conflict is ready to be tackled—that it is, in professional parlance, ripe for resolution.

Ensuring conflict ripeness is presented here as the third step in the mediation process, but it actually consists of two activities—assessing ripeness and enhancing ripeness—that will probably be initiated at different times: assessment early on, while the conflict as a whole is being assessed, and enhancement later, once the mediator has determined that he or she is ready and able to tackle this conflict. Once begun, however, both activities will run in tandem, with the mediator adjusting his or her enhancement strategy in line with the conflict's fluctuating level of ripeness.

Phases of escalation, de-escalation, or stalemate in a conflict's life cycle call for distinct mediation approaches. Some approaches address mounting risks, others address unsustainable burdens or sunk costs. The parties' trust in a mediator pursuing any approach will be colored by the outcomes of previous mediation attempts. Some earlier attempts, even if ultimately unsuccessful, may have established a foundation for future negotiations. Earlier outright failures or abandoned attempts, by contrast, may have left legacies of suspicion and cynicism.

Assess Ripeness

Many mediation studies give considerable attention to the concept of conflict ripeness. A conflict may become ripe for negotiation when antagonists recognize that they are in a mutually hurting stalemate and sense that a way out is possible. Both sides become aware they cannot defeat the enemy outright and that continued violence not only will be costly and ineffective but will risk weakening their situation. A related conceptualization of ripeness is the moment when antagonists recognize their interdependence and that important goals cannot be achieved without the other side. The two sides must also have a sense that some mutually acceptable settlement formula is available to them.

> **Determine whether parties believe they have reached a mutually hurting stalemate.**
>
> **Confirm that parties can deliver on agreements.**
>
> **Assess internal political and public support for peace.**

Parties not only must perceive the stalemate to be painful but also must be strong and coherent enough to make decisions and deliver on them.

Finally, for ripeness to be complete, there must be strong support for a peace process among both internal political actors and the public.

In 1989, the FMLN and the government of El Salvador recognized that their respective military efforts were costly and would be unsuccessful. The outlines of a mutually satisfactory peace agreement also became evident, and serious negotiations mediated by Alvaro de Soto on behalf of the United Nations commenced in 1990.

Enhance Ripeness

A mediator should make judgments about how best to intervene to help ripen the conflict and to create a readiness to negotiate among the parties. Effective mediators convince parties (particularly those actors with decision-making power or influence in the conflict) that goals cannot be achieved through continued violence and that other means are possible and practical. A mediator may follow several paths of persuasion in the effort to induce a change in antagonists' perspectives.

Help Elites Understand Costs and Benefits

Elites may be relatively insulated from the costs and consequences of violence. Credible third parties can increase elite awareness by providing information and documentation and sharing analyses. Even familiar facts become more convincing or less deniable when presented by a new actor. Patterns of interdependence can also be explored and explained.

Mediators may also educate elites about lost opportunities or potential benefits of conflict termination, offering different scenarios or introducing feasible alternatives and the possibility of sharing burdens. Education can help elites recalculate the costs of continued conflict and see the benefits of searching for peace.

The prospect of losing substantial amounts of international financial assistance was a jointly recognized factor that brought pressure on the two parties to the conflict in Kenya in 2008.

- **Use credible third parties to inform elites of the costs of continued violence.**
- **Explore and explain patterns of interdependence.**
- **Educate elites about the benefits of ending the conflict.**

Increase Pressure on Elites through Accountability

Recalcitrant actors may pursue violent conflict despite its costs to society. Direct personal costs can be increased if actors understand they will be held accountable for their actions. Mediators can promote accountability in a number of ways. The first involves appealing to transcendent or locally legitimate principles (e.g., patriotic duty, responsibility to the people, a leader's place in history). Mediators may make this case directly or may offer platforms to locally acknowledged voices of moral, cultural, or religious authority to make such arguments to elites.

- **Determine if promoting accountability will further the peace process.**
- **If elites are not to be held accountable, understand and address the implications.**

Mediators may also use formal institutions and practices to promote accountability. This might include gathering evidence regarding human rights abuses or corruption for the purposes of documenting and publicizing leadership failings. This evidence may also be used in judicial review, if not in local courts then via transnational jurisdictions or international tribunals. Mediators may choose to utilize third-party advocates or experts.

A third avenue for fostering elite accountability is to turn an international spotlight on the conflict, perhaps via media attention or the involvement of international organizations, NGOs, or international solidarity groups. All these avenues bring pressure on elites to appreciate the costs of their continued commitment to the pursuit of violence.

An alternative approach is not to hold elites accountable. If obdurate elites are an obstacle to peace, then granting them impunity (in the form of amnesty, asylum, or the promise not to prosecute) may be a step toward getting parties to the negotiating table. However, granting impunity risks compromising justice for the sake of peace, which can create challenges for acceptance and implementation of an agreement. If granting impunity is among the tactics used, a mediator must decide how to limit any deleterious consequences on the peace process and its outcome, perhaps by using alternative mechanisms for transitional justice.

A qualified approach to amnesty was incorporated in the creation of South Africa's Truth and Reconciliation Commission, which provided criminal and civil amnesty to individuals in exchange for full confessions. Individuals who did not confess their crimes were subject to prosecution, and information from other confessions could be used in such prosecutions.

Cultivate Leaders Who Can Assume Responsibility for Negotiations

If top leaders are unwilling to negotiate, are other potential leaders more amenable to entering negotiations? Attention from a mediator can raise the stature of such potential leaders; communications can help build new coalitions of support for a peace process. However, such efforts risk backfiring if they appear manipulative. Mediators must work with leaders who possess internal legitimacy and support.

Create Balance between Parties

Another way to create a stalemate and foster readiness to negotiate is to strengthen the weaker side in a conflict, helping to create an objective balance of power. This may include helping the weaker side by providing material resources or by encouraging it to think through strategies, build coalitions, and find advocates and allies.

The international community had to provide logistical support to the rebel group RENAMO in order for its leaders to be full participants in the Mozambique peace process.

Change the Costs and Benefits of the Conflict

In order to persuade leaders to change their calculation vis-à-vis costs and benefits of pursuing the conflict, is it possible to change the actual costs and benefits? A mediator with the resources to do so may induce antagonists to turn to negotiation through a variety of means that change the context of the conflict. These include the threat or imposition of sanctions (e.g., travel restrictions, financial sanctions, arms embargoes, and trade embargoes, especially on conflict commodities such as diamonds or timber) as well as the offer of aid, the provision of reconstruction programs, or the commitment of outside parties to guarantee a peace settlement.

Take into Account the Legacies of Previous Mediation Attempts

Much can be learned from previous efforts to mediate the conflict at hand and from efforts to mediate other conflicts, especially conflicts in the same region or with similar causes. In addition to examining case studies and maintaining familiarity with the mediation literature more broadly, the mediator can learn much from interviews with other mediators, their support staff, and others with firsthand experience of previous mediation initiatives.

Assess Positive and Negative Results of Previous Efforts

Previous interrupted or unsuccessful attempts at mediation affect subsequent initiatives and cannot be ignored. A mediator should understand the legacies of previous mediation efforts before embarking on a new one.

On the one hand, there may be something to build upon, including negotiation skills conferred, relationships forged, or mechanisms established. Rather than squandering previous accomplishments, subsequent mediations should attempt to harness these.

In the 1990s, when conditions were finally ripe for a settlement of the Ecuador-Peru border dispute, mediators were able to use the four-country guarantor structure established by the 1942 Rio Protocol. In the intervening years, the four guarantors had grown accustomed to dealing with the problem, and Peru and Ecuador had come to recognize and welcome their authority.

On the other hand, unsuccessful peace processes can promote conflict intractability. Failed negotiations may leave parties convinced of the futility of talks and with a more intransigent view of opponents. Partiality or incompetence on the part of previous negotiators may have generated suspicion and distrust of subsequent mediators. After unsuccessful talks, associated reasonable proposals may become discredited and deemed intrinsically flawed. Unimplemented settlements may raise general cynicism and discourage potential donors and allies from supporting a process.

Consider New Sequencing of Decisions, New Settlement Formulas, and New Actors

If previous attempts have failed, what can a new mediator do? An important first step is to acknowledge that the failure is now part of the conflict history and to analyze the failure with the parties to develop a shared understanding of what happened and to renew trust in mediators and mediation. Other steps include sequencing decisions differently than in the earlier process or introducing new settlement formulas. New actors—not only new individual mediators but new types of mediators—may also be able to make progress. If a previous Track-I attempt failed, perhaps a weak mediator is needed to reopen lines of communication. If the earlier unsuccessful attempt was Track-II, perhaps the conflict now calls for the full public commitment of Track-I actors.

Whether earlier efforts to launch a peace process have been outright failures or partial successes, the information, perspectives, insights, and experience generated by those earlier endeavors should be absorbed by the new mediator.

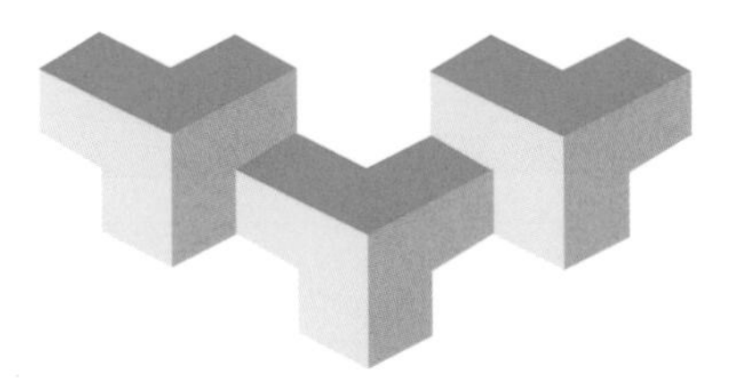

STEP FOUR

Conduct Track-I Mediation

Once the mediator has assessed the conflict, determined his or her readiness to act and evaluated and, if necessary, enhanced ripeness, the mediator is ready to begin the fourth stage of the process: negotiation. Among the tasks that fall to the mediator at this stage are laying the groundwork, creating roles for all relevant actors, handling logistics, actually conducting negotiations, fitting the public into the process, and working with the media.

Use Consultations and Prenegotiations to Lay the Groundwork

Solicit Input and Build Trust

Regardless of the specific structure of the negotiations, participants are more apt to be satisfied with the outcome if they have been consulted in its design. Rather than independently reviewing and choosing from among available designs and then presenting the parties with that choice, mediators should solicit the parties' input early on: what form should the meetings take, where should they be held, whether and how to record them, how broad should the agenda be. Consultations are an opportunity to build trust. Reporting back to those who have been consulted is also important, especially if the mediator has asked the parties to respond to formal queries (e.g., surveys and questionnaires). Participants who are not completely satisfied with the final design will be more likely to endorse it if they have been consulted.

Topics for Prenegotiation

Preliminary "talks about talks" should establish shared expectations and agreements on a number of matters, including the following:

- structure and format of talks: for example, large-scale conference, summit of key representatives, roundtable discussion, shuttle mediation, bilateral talks
- decision rule: for example, simple majority, two-thirds majority, consensus, unanimity, via secret votes, open show of hands
- guidelines for participation: for example, who qualifies as an appropriate participant, what constitutes appropriate and representative levels of participation, how to ensure representation of those not directly at the table
- communication: for example, method of recording the process, confidentiality, closed or open meetings, progress reports, handling the media, reporting back to constituents
- timeframe, schedule, pacing
- acceptable procedures to handle sticking points
- role of mediator(s): for example, convener, facilitator, Track-I or Track-II or both

Establish Clear Ground Rules

Trust and confidence among the parties can be fostered by clear and consistently applied ground rules for negotiations. Involving participants in designing those ground rules is itself an exercise in building trust.

That being said, much of the work of international mediation is conducted informally, often with only one partner and without rules and guidelines of this sort. When serendipity and emerging opportunities present themselves, the mediator should adjust strategies and arrangements accordingly.

Determine Participants

While a large number of stakeholders will be consulted, relatively few will participate in direct negotiations. When helping to determine whom to involve in direct negotiations, the mediator should consider the most viable partners, be prepared to manage spoilers, and try to include marginalized groups as appropriate.

Work with Viable Partners

The mediator should work with viable partners who have sufficient control over the drivers of violence and relevant constituencies. Generally, this means working with top-level leaders, but the mediator should not focus only on senior leaders; midlevel leaders can be viable (and sometimes invaluable) partners, too.

- **Choose partners who have sufficient control over drivers of conflict and relevant constituencies.**
- **Engage both top-level and mid-level leaders; recognize their strengths and limitations.**

Top-Level Leaders. Negotiations often involve the top leaders of each party or their direct representatives. A high profile, however, can constrain top leaders, who, if they appear to be accepting less than publicly stated goals, risk both their own positions and the interests of their constituencies. High status confers the power to negotiate but may also reduce the freedom to negotiate.

Midlevel Leaders. Midlevel leaders play a useful role in many negotiations. They know and are known by the top leaders, yet have broader connections to constituencies. Their positions and effectiveness depend less on a having a high public profile, and they thus enjoy greater maneuverability. Negotiating teams should generally include midlevel leaders with varied areas of expertise and different links to constituents.

Manage Spoilers

Spoilers, who will block settlements if their own interests are not met, require careful management. To give a seat to a spoiler may appear to be rewarding bad behavior, and may risk alienating other participants and tainting the talks. Yet outright exclusion often means they will use their power to resist both the peace process and its

- **Involve spoilers in the process.**
- **If spoilers continue to impede the process, find ways to marginalize or undercut them.**

outcome. Furthermore, their exclusion risks eliminating from negotiations the very actors and issues that are most difficult to deal with, thus undercutting the realism of the mediation effort. Consequently, instead of excluding spoilers, mediators should find ways to marginalize or undercut them while also involving them in the process—for instance, via meetings with mediators rather than with the other parties or by including them as individuals without conferring a public role or formal standing.

Steven Stedman has presented a typology of spoiler management based on an analysis of the spoilers' key characteristics (e.g., whether they are positioned inside or outside the peace process, their numbers, whether their goals are total or limited, and the nature of their power bases). Stedman recommends using one or a combination of three strategies: inducement, socialization, and coercion.

➤ *Inducement* involves taking positive measures to address the grievances of factions that obstruct peace. When spoilers act out of fear, they will usually demand some sort of physical protection. When acting out of a sense of fairness, they will usually demand material benefits. When acting out of a sense of justice, they tend to demand recognition or legitimacy. However, when used inappropriately, inducement can exacerbate the problem.

When the UN mission in Cambodia tried to use a strategy of inducement, it backfired, strengthening the state of Cambodia while weakening the opposition party participating in the peace process.

➤ *A socialization* strategy establishes a set of norms for acceptable behaviors by parties that commit to peace or seek to join a peace process. Adherence to these norms is encouraged by the use of carrots and sticks. The norms must be clearly established and communicated to all stakeholders and must remain consistent over time.

The management of RENAMO by the UN mission in Mozambique is an example of a successful socialization strategy. It included constant persuasion and peacebrokering as well as practical logistics for assembly, demobilization, and disarmament.

➤ A *coercion* strategy relies on the threat of punishment if a spoiler does not fall into line. Coercion can take the form of threats, the use of force, warnings that the peace process will go forward with or without the spoiler (the "departing-train" strategy), and the mediator's withdrawal from the peace process.

The UN mission in Cambodia successfully used the departing-train strategy in dealing with the Khmer Rouge in 1992–93.

For spoilers who pursue total power and whose goals are not subject to change, the use of force or the departing-train strategy are usually the only effective strategies. Inducement may be useful for spoilers with more limited goals, but only if their grievances are acceptable to the other stakeholders; otherwise, some level of socialization or coercion may be necessary. However, inducement should never be used with a greedy spoiler, whose goals expand and contract with calculations of cost and risk, as it is likely to simply whet the spoiler's appetite for further grievances. Depending on the context, some coercion may be necessary, but long-term socialization is the only truly effective strategy for greedy spoilers.

Include Marginalized Groups in Negotiations

In addition to combatants or other parties central to the conflict, the key stakeholders in society ideally should have seats at the table. Typically, they will include representatives of civil society (whether or not these are formal organizations); women; and ethnic, religious, or ideological minorities, who are often marginalized in decision making. If combatants are opposed to their inclusion, as is usually the case, the mediator may opt to consult informally with civil society or minority representatives in the initial stages of negotiation, providing them with a formal seat in later stages. (Other options are explored in the discussion below of public involvement.)

The Advantages of Women's Participation

Women's experience of war (as combatants or civilians) and of peace is often better heard and better put on the table by women mediators or by women they involve in the mediation process. Women often lead civil society organizations and are critical to the public acceptance and implementation of peace settlements. Moreover, ensuring that women participate in designing the ground rules of a peace process increases the chances of their effective participation in that process, both at the negotiating table and in public fora.

Arrange Logistics

Provide a Safe, Effective, and Well-Resourced Working Environment

Effective mediators provide a safe working environment that accords no unfair advantage to any side and enables effective exchange. Arranging and paying for the components of such an environment is essential to any mediation. These components include the following:

- a secure, accessible venue that is not identified with any party to the conflict
- security, transportation, meals, housing, and meeting space (including space for private meetings within each party and informal sharing of views between parties)
- visas and identity papers (including documents for participants who may be outlawed or traveling under aliases)
- proven translators who are independent of both parties
- skilled staff who are sensitive to protocol and cross-cultural issues, and who can provide technical expertise and help draft agreements
- agreed-upon mechanisms for recording proceedings
- reliable and secure means of communication (between mediators and their institutional base as well as between all negotiators and their counselors and constituents)
- the means to handle press inquiries

It should be noted that the interactions between parties will not always be formal affairs conducted around a negotiating table. In fact, in many negotiations the parties do not even meet each other but instead interact solely through the mediator.

Manage Information Effectively

The provision of high-quality supporting materials (such as maps) and expertise on a range of important topics (especially technical ones such as military issues, boundary demarcation, and property issues) can be essential in maintaining momentum when specific questions arise and in developing concrete options.

> **Provide supporting materials and expertise.**

> **Keep good records of the negotiations.**

No less important is scrupulous recordkeeping of the negotiating process. These records can provide benchmarks of progress made; improve the mediator's understanding of the parties and their negotiating strategies; enable evaluation after the process is complete; and prevent subsequent disagreements between the parties—and even the mediator—about exactly what the parties agreed to during the negotiations.

Develop and Execute Strategies for Advancing Negotiations

During negotiations, a mediator must deploy numerous specific skills (such as convening, facilitating, and reframing) to accomplish numerous tasks, including cultivating confidence, disaggregating and sequencing decisions, developing and assessing options, breaking deadlocks, and communicating with constituents.

> **Develop trust.**

> **Establish an environment and channels that facilitate communication.**

> **Create momentum through confidence-building measures and joint activities.**

Increase Parties' Trust and Confidence

Facilitating mediation includes not only providing a venue but also creating and maintaining an environment conducive to constructive negotiations. Key tasks include developing trust among participants and establishing channels for communication between them to support negotiations. If the level of trust is high enough, the parties can be brought together, in which case care must be taken to establish a "safe space" for communication. Participants in such a space must be able to talk freely without being subject to attack. They also need to be encouraged to listen attentively to the other side and to look for areas of commonalities, not just differences. The mediator needs to accommodate different communication styles and to help participants understand each other and communicate effectively, even when their styles differ.

If the level of trust is too low to bring the parties together, shuttle diplomacy may be the best option. In this case, the mediator can go back and forth between the parties, identifying issues, interests, options, and offers. This is a slow process, but sometimes it is safer than bringing the parties face to face.

In this effort, the mediator may also need to help each side recognize that the other side has legitimate grievances. In his book *Statecraft: And How to Restore America's Standing in the World*, Dennis Ross suggests that the mediator do this by demonstrating first how well he or she understands the grievances of the side with whom he or she is talking and then to treat the other side's concerns in relation to that context. Ross also argues that the mediator must help the sides abandon their mythologies—especially illusory self-images—and adopt more realistic expectations about the accommodations necessary for a settlement.

As relationships begin to develop, the mediator can create momentum by persuading the parties to adopt confidence-building measures such as making reciprocal gestures related to humanitarian issues or softening the tone of their public statements. Joint study groups and workshops are also opportunities to build relationships. The inclusion of allies, partners, and civil society actors (e.g., from the business community, academic institutions, and religious bodies) helps to surround the parties with a sense of public support and responsibility.

Use Multiple Tactics to Facilitate Agreement

- **Select appropriate tactics.**
- **Consider breaking down issues into manageable segments.**
- **Consider linking issues to increase buy-in.**
- **Sequence decisions so as to build momentum.**

The tactics a mediator uses will vary depending on the circumstances and overall mediation strategy. If not already done during the prenegotiation stage, the mediator needs to begin by working with the parties to determine what the scope of the negotiations will be: what topics will be on the table, what topics will not, and in what sequence subjects will be negotiated.

It is vital to break down peace negotiations, which are often overwhelmingly complex, into more manageable segments and deal with them in sequence. Large and difficult issues can be disaggregated into smaller issues.

Those issues can then be considered not by the parties' entire negotiating teams but by subcommittees or outside working groups, which subsequently report back to the teams. This approach is especially useful in resolving factual disputes, but it can also be used to brainstorm options for settlement.

This tactic was effectively employed in the process that generated the Comprehensive Peace Agreement that ended the civil war between north and south in Sudan, with separate working groups being created to discuss security, power sharing, and wealth sharing.

Conversely, some cases may call for linking one issue with another to increase the likelihood of buy-in. For example, it might be best to negotiate the terms of a cease-fire in the context of agreement on other critical issues so that if a party feels itself shortchanged on the cease-fire, it can get much of what it wants on other issues in contention.

How a mediator sequences discussions and decisions is also extremely important. This may entail dealing with the easiest issues first, to build momentum and confidence. Conversely, it may call for tackling the most contentious issues first, while initial commitment is strong or because smaller issues cannot be resolved without knowing how the larger issues will be resolved. An appropriate order will depend on context. Adopting any method of sequencing is preferable to seeing talks stall or collapse under the pressure of trying to address all questions simultaneously.

Introduce Fresh Frameworks

One way of keeping negotiations moving is to persuade parties to frame issues in terms not of *positions,* which are often in opposition to each other, but of *interests, needs, and ultimate goals* which are often compatible or even mutually supportive (e.g., increasing the security of one side often increases the security of the other). Once interests, needs, and ultimate goals are understood, mediators should highlight any areas of commonality and help the parties brainstorm options for resolving disagreements.

- **Help parties identify interests, needs, and ultimate goals.**
- **Highlight shared goals.**
- **Use proven techniques to break impasses.**

When they get stuck, mediators can ask participants to work back from possible futures rather than forward from current problems. Stories and metaphors, humor, and even training-type exercises can be effective tools to get participants to see their situation—and each other—in a new light. Contingent agreements and matched conditional commitments ("yes, if") can be used to define elements of a settlement and create incentives for compliance. The mediator may introduce new settlement formulas that include new actors to serve as reliable guarantors, thus spreading the political risk of a settlement.

The IGAD mediation of the Sudan civil war became much more effective when the United States and three other nations were brought in as guarantors.

Encourage Communication with Constituencies

Communication and consultation with constituencies increase the chance that a settlement—even one that is disappointing in some respects—will be accepted as fair and supported by the public on both sides. To this end, the mediator should encourage negotiators to inform and consult their constituencies, learning from them what terms are likely to be acceptable and what will be seen as unacceptable. Negotiators should also report on the progress of negotiations and the terms being discussed, thereby building support for a settlement. Such communication reduces the danger of a top-down settlement being rejected when it is announced, or undercut during its implementation.

Some observers believe that the various Israeli-Palestinian peace initiatives would have been successful if negotiators and mediators had recognized the respective interests of religious constituencies on both sides and engaged them in the peace process.

Use Different Types of Leverage to Encourage Compromise

Mediators should review the potential sources of leverage identified during step 1 (conflict assessment) and determine which can actually be brought to bear on the parties. Typically, mediators can bring some or all of the following types of leverage to the negotiating table:

- reward power, when the mediator has something to offer to the parties in exchange for changes in behavior
- coercive power that relies on threats and sanctions, and includes military options

- expert power that is based on the mediator's knowledge and experience with certain issues
- legitimate power that is based on certain rights and legally sanctioned authority under international law
- referent power that is based on a desire of the parties to the conflict to maintain a valued relationship with the mediator
- informational power that works on the content of the information conveyed as in the case of a go-between or message carrier

Specific resources within these categories depend on the mediator's institutional readiness, mandate, and resources.

- **Identify and apply appropriate leverage.**
- **Increase leverage through coalitions and allies.**
- **Apply incentives and coercion in combination.**
- **Use conditionality, but avoid rewarding intransigence.**
- **Never bluff.**

A mediator can increase and multiply these sources of leverage by using coalitions and allies.

During the implementation phase of the peace agreement in Mozambique, Aldo Ajello, the UN secretary-general's special representative for Mozambique, was able to exercise significant leverage because of the relationships he established with key embassies in Mozambique. Ajello not only kept the ambassadors of France, Portugal, the United Kingdom, and the United States informed of what he was planning to do but also involved them in the decision-making process; as a consequence, he enjoyed their support and was able to deploy a variety of resources they made available.

Mediators should be aware of how their use of leverage will impact the parties and the dynamics of the conflict. Incentives and coercion are most effective when applied in combination, not only because they present a more compelling offer but because of the effect on the negotiating dynamic. Threats and coercion generate resistance that can be offset by incentives that foster cooperation.

The type of leverage used should be appropriate for addressing underlying sources of conflict and the reluctance of the parties to settle.

In the peace process for El Salvador, the U.S. government helped to erode opposition to the process among wealthy landholders by subsidizing the land transfer program.

Incentives or deterrents must also have sufficient value to induce changes in behavior without being so excessive that they inflate future demands.

Conditionality may be used to link progress on an issue with rewards. Mediators should avoid the appearance of rewarding intransigence by creating a process in which rewards are delivered in response to specific commitments and actions from a party.

Mediators should never bluff or use threats unless the ability and political will to carry them out exists.

Engage the Public and Media

Develop Channels for Public Involvement

- **Consider giving civil society stakeholders a seat at the table.**
- **Consider using parallel meetings with civil society stakeholders.**
- **Promote communication with the public.**

Public participation in the negotiations in some form is imperative; after all, the ultimate responsibility for resolving a conflict lies within the local society. Public participation is also strategically sound, as participants are far more apt than spectators to support and sustain a settlement.

Context will determine the best means of incorporating the public. For example, the more representative and accountable the parties have been, the less important it is that civil society actors have a seat at the table and vice versa.

Public involvement can take many forms.

At the Table. Civil society stakeholders may be directly engaged, particularly those from representative organizations with experience or expertise on specific issues. They may be important assets in working groups addressing issues relevant to their constituencies. By being engaged, such actors provide a counterweight to elites and potential spoilers and ensure that broader public interests are negotiated. They may also be very effective at explaining the negotiating process to constituents. Resistance by the combatants to the direct involvement of these actors, however, may require alternative means of inclusion.

Parallel Meetings. Conducting parallel consultative meetings for civil society can help legitimize and sustain formal talks without making formal talks unwieldy. Such meetings may provide additional bargaining power for negotiators voicing civil society's interest. They also present an opportunity for civil society to practice democratic procedures.

Two-Way Communication. Another way to incorporate the public is by instituting some form of two-way communication. News of negotiations should reach the public, and public discussion and reactions should be heard by negotiators. The means of such communication could include discussion forums, workshops, opinion polls, and referenda.

None of these methods is without risk. Broad engagement can make negotiations unwieldy or unfocused. Parallel meetings could be hijacked by elite groups to promote their own, narrow interests. An informed civil society may reject delicate agreements reached by elites or may conclude that talks are not addressing their own concerns.

Manage Media and Public Relations

During a mediation effort, a media strategy that extends beyond responding to press questions is essential. The strategy should take into account the role that the media has played thus far in the conflict; any legacy of hate media or propaganda must be addressed. At the same time, the mediator should work with the media to reduce inflammatory or biased news coverage. Confidentiality may be an important aspect of talks, yet the lack of information is a vacuum that someone will fill, perhaps with rumors, fears, or slander. The mediator should encourage the parties to make joint public appearances, which will model the progress of negotiations while reducing the ability of the parties to spin public announcements to their own benefit.

A good communication and public relations strategy will aim not just to explain isolated events but also to educate the public about the path to peace. The mediator will usually have natural local allies in the effort to build support for the peace process. These allies can be empowered by cultivating press freedom and peace media (including popular forms such as community publishing, interactive websites, and social networks using mobile phones).

STEP FIVE

Encourage Track-II Dialogue

There is a growing consensus among both official and unofficial actors that no single actor or activity is sufficient to build sustainable peace in situations of complex conflict, and that the achievement of that goal requires both top-down and bottom-up approaches. Track-II, or unofficial, diplomacy conducted among grassroots and midlevel opinion leaders can be a valuable adjunct to the formal peace negotiations. Track-II efforts can help the local community engage in the kinds of tasks and make the necessary psychological changes required to generate and sustain support for a peace process. They also can generate ideas and issues that should be included in the negotiation process.

Track-II efforts can also play a constructive role even before a conflict becomes ripe for Track-I efforts; for instance, Track-II practitioners can float low-profile, low-risk "trial balloons" to gauge support for possible subsequent Track-I mediation efforts.

In Tajikistan, the unofficial Inter-Tajik Dialogue met for thirteen months prior to the commencement of official negotiations in 1994, during which time it helped set the agenda for official talks and demonstrated that progress could be made at the official level. Once official negotiations began, those involved in the unofficial dialogue focused on building support for the official process and strategizing about how to promote national reconciliation.

Track-II participants need to understand at all times that they are an adjunct to the Track-I process and cannot replace that process. Moreover, efforts must be made to coordinate Track-II efforts, not just with Track-I endeavors, but with each other, to enhance synergies and avoid confusion and congestion.

Identify and Coordinate with Track-II Efforts

Ascertain Status and Potential of Track-II Efforts

The Track-I mediator should ascertain the existence and status of ongoing Track-II efforts and decide if and how to communicate, coordinate, or even work with those endeavors. Some Track-II activities may complicate or undercut the work of the official mediator, and the mediator should seek to minimize their disruptive potential, but others may help the mediator and should be encouraged and supported. The mediator will probably be most concerned about any disruptive effects of Track-II efforts once the Track-I negotiations are under way, but the mediator should be attentive to both the negative and the positive potential of Track-II endeavors throughout the entire mediation process.

Focus on Track-II Activities that Build Parties' Capacity and Foster Wider Support for the Process

The Track-II activities most relevant to a Track-I mediator are those that either build the parties' capacity to participate effectively and to reach a settlement or build support for the peace process in the wider community. To be most effective, capacity building for the parties should be coordinated with the Track-I process to target specific needs identified by the official mediator, such as negotiation skills, coalition building, or platform development. Track-II processes aimed at building wider support for the process should engage members of elite subgroups with ties to official negotiators, as well as leaders who represent significant sections of the public, especially those sections not directly involved in the Track-I process.

Promote Cooperation between Tracks

Share Information and Clarify Roles

Ideally, coordination between the two tracks will occur both during the mediation process and toward its end, when Track-I mediators may need to hand off some of the responsibilities for implementation to Track-II actors. Whenever possible, Track-I mediators should meet with the major Track-II groups to share information and analysis (to the extent possible, given confidentiality restrictions) and use this information as a basis for agreeing on explicit Track-I and Track-II roles for facilitating the peace process. At a minimum, mediators should work to develop shared visions of mutually reinforcing activities that can guide each group's involvement.

In the long term, enhanced coordination and cooperation depend upon regular communication between Track-I and Track-II professionals. One mechanism to promote a close relationship is to convene regular forums for practitioners working in specific conflict areas.

Such forums have been established in the cases of the Georgian-Abkahz conflict and the effort to reconstruct Afghanistan.

A decentralized planning model, in which people meet frequently to share the latest news, analyze and strategize together, and, where appropriate, take joint action, is very effective. Field-based representatives of Track-I and Track-II organizations may coordinate more efficiently than their geographically scattered organizational leaderships.

Reward Track-II Efforts that Further the Track-I Process

Although a Track-I mediator cannot regulate all the relevant Track-II activities, he or she can exercise some control over the access that those activities have to the Track-I process, rewarding those efforts that have the potential to support it. Such support could range from occasional briefings to keep Track-II actors informed of progress to active collaboration on aspects of the mediation.

Track-I interveners in the Moldovan-Transdniestrian conflict discussed broad plans with the Track-II Moldovan Initiative Committee on Management, leading to a study visit to Northern Ireland for the parties and the Track-I mediators.

Maintain the Independence of Track-II Initiatives

Cooperation must not go so far as to blur the distinction between the two tracks, however. Track-II organizations need to maintain their separation and distance from Track-I; after all, one of the big advantages of Track-II is that, because it is seen as more independent, it can do things that Track-I cannot.

Examples of Track-II Support for Track-I

Facilitation of Unofficial Negotiations
Facilitate unofficial meetings with either Track-I or Track-II leaders to explore options or to float trial balloons or model peace plans for an official process.

Capacity Building for Negotiating Parties
Provide training in negotiating and conflict resolution skills, and in platform/ alliance development.

Interactive Problem Solving
Conduct workshops before or in parallel with Track-I mediation to investigate underlying interests and to develop mutual understanding.

Logistical Support for Track-I
Provide Track-I efforts with technical expertise, additional staff, and logistical, administrative, or infrastructure support.

Negotiation and Mediation of Subsidiary and Local Issues
Facilitate resolution of lower-level disputes within the context of the wider Track-I process.

Early Warning
Provide independent insights into the nature of the conflict and identify emerging problems and opportunities.

Capacity Building for Civil Society and the Wider Population
Improve the ability of citizens to participate effectively in the peace process by fostering understanding of the peace process; initiate programs in support of the institution and state-building necessary for sustainable peace.

Reconciliation and Relationship Building
Facilitate dialogues with civil society to build relationships that foster intercommunal trust and communication and support long-term peace.

Transitional Steps
Undertake programs to assist with disarmament, demobilization, and reintegration of combatants; participate in transitional justice efforts.

Implementation Support
Mobilize and educate the population to monitor and participate in the peace process, including security support such as neighborhood watch or disarmament programs.

STEP SIX

Construct a Peace Agreement

The sixth and final step in the mediation process is constructing an agreement that is acceptable not only to the parties to the conflict but also to the wider public, and that stands a good chance of being implemented successfully.

Develop a Declaration of Principles

Obtain Agreement on Basic Principles

Prior to the development of final agreements, it is often helpful to have the parties agree to a "declaration of basic principles" or a negotiating framework that provides the overarching structure for a subsequently drafted, detailed peace agreement. This negotiating framework usually includes statements such as:

- The parties seek to live together in peace.
- The rights of states and/or nations and peoples will be protected.
- All parties will be treated with respect.

Craft the Broad Outlines of an Agreement

The framework also usually contains the broad outlines of an agreement: Side X will do A, B, and C, if Side Y does D, E, and F. These agreements are stated in general terms, acceptable both to the parties at the table and to the political leaders and the general public. Determining exactly what these general ideas mean in practice and how they will be achieved is the next, very challenging part of the job.

The Declaration of Principles signed by the SPLM and the Government of Sudan set the framework for the subsequent peace negotiations, which brought an end to the North-South civil war.

Assemble a Peace Agreement

Determine a Drafting Process

Most agreements are drafted in one of two ways. One approach is the "single-text" negotiating process in which the mediator listens to the suggestions of both sides and drafts a proposed agreement that best meets each sides' needs and interests. This single text is then edited—either simultaneously or sequentially—by the parties until a draft acceptable to all sides is attained.

The other approach is for each side to simultaneously produce its own draft agreement; the mediator then takes these agreements and, working with the parties, tries to mesh them together into one document that eventually everyone can agree on.

The drafting process can take place as the negotiations proceed, with discrete parts of an agreement being drafted as soon as individual issues have been resolved; alternatively, the entire agreement can be drafted at the end, after all the issues have been negotiated and all the trade-offs between issues have been made. Both approaches have advantages, but if the issues are negotiated separately and the agreement is drafted in sections, it often is necessary to specify at the outset that "nothing is agreed until everything is agreed." This prevents negotiators from "cherry picking"—taking the agreements they want and discarding the ones they don't want. It also allows some flexibility for rewriting sections later, should trade-offs between issues become apparent that were not evident before.

Translate Principles into Legally Binding Language

Changing a declaration of principles into an actual agreement is often an arduous task that takes weeks—if not months or even years—of negotiation over the details. Each general statement has to be spelled out in legal terms so that it is clear to both sides exactly what is expected of whom and when each action is to be accomplished.

Components of a Peace Agreement

Although the components of a peace agreement will vary greatly from case to case, some provisions are fairly universal:

- security guarantees
- demilitarization, demobilization, and reintegration of fighters
- protection of all parties' human rights
- return or resettlement of refugees and internally displaced persons (IDPs)
- social, political, legal, and economic restructuring
- settlement of border disputes
- nature of transitional government
- elections
- implementation strategies
- timetables

Incorporate Strategies for Implementation and Monitoring

One key to fashioning a successful agreement is to write into that agreement strategies for implementation and for monitoring and (if possible) enforcing compliance with the terms of the agreement. It needs to be clear who is to do what by when, how performance is to be measured and by whom, and what will happen if targets are not reached. When these specifics are left vague, one or both sides can too easily procrastinate or evade their responsibilities. (Further approaches to implementation are discussed below.)

Plan for Implementation

Peace settlements have to be implementable. Overly ambitious agreements that do not attract the resources, skills, and commitment to enforce them do damage by disillusioning the parties and encouraging the view that violence is the only feasible route to the decisive achievement of their goals.

Peace is made by people, not by settlements. Thus, the parties to the conflict, affected societies, and external partners must be mobilized to undertake implementation, from planning and managing to monitoring and enforcing. Implementation plans should anticipate both the immediate transitions out of violence and long-term post-conflict peacebuilding.

Make the Local Population Stakeholders and Guarantors of the Agreement

Peace settlements should include local community members as planners, agents, managers, and monitors of implementation. Tapping into local knowledge, networks, and leadership increases the resources available for implementation, builds social capital, and solidifies local ownership, increasing civil society's stake in the implementation.

While implementation tasks should not go beyond the technical, managerial, and personnel capacities of the local community, full participation in the process can expand such skills and capacities. Implementation frameworks should therefore include local input in planning and design, optimize use of local resources in implementation, and incorporate means to provide progress reports and evaluations to the community.

A successful and durable peace will be more likely if society is fully mobilized to implement the settlement benchmarks. The local business community can be directly involved in the economic reintegration of combatants; traditional justice mechanisms or religious practices can be adapted to enable reconciliation; local materials and labor can be utilized in reconstruction; local human rights monitors can help safeguard returning refugees; local stewards can keep watch to prevent corruption and waste; and local media can keep the community informed about all these practices. Societal actors should be involved in ways that make them stakeholders and guarantors of the agreement instead of passive onlookers.

Use Metrics to Gauge Progress

Metrics—or measurable indicators of progress—can assist in formulating and implementing a peace agreement. More particularly, metrics help ensure the mediator and parties establish realistic goals, bring adequate resources and authorities to bear, focus their efforts strategically, and enhance prospects for attaining an enduring resolution of the conflict. It is important during the peace process to collect baseline data to aid in diagnosing potential obstacles prior to a settlement. During implementation, it is equally important to track progress from the point of the settlement through to sustained peace. The most valuable metrics must measure outcomes essential to implementation of the agreement—that is, they measure results and impact rather than level of effort.

- **Identify metrics that gauge impact not level of activity.**
- **Collect just baseline data.**
- **Track progress throughout implementation.**

In Northern Ireland, measuring progress in the "decommissioning" (i.e., the effective destruction) of weapons in the IRA's arsenal has been critical to achieving peace. In Kosovo, the UN mission developed a set of metrics to assess progress toward meeting standards in eight core areas of governance and human rights that had to be met before the international community would initiate a diplomatic process aimed at resolving the issue of Kosovo's political status.

Design Dispute Resolution Mechanisms

During the period of transition out of conflict, settlements are bound to falter. Implementation designs should include mechanisms to review progress and handle problems. Roundtables, implementation councils, or joint committees should be available to hear grievances, mediate disputes, and make adjustments in implementation. The establishment of a monitoring and conflict resolution mechanism by the parties to the accord may be sufficient.

Use External Parties to Support Implementation

External partners provide assurance, resources, expertise, and experience in support of the implementation of peace settlements. But they also have their own interests that may conflict with the mediator's goals.

Third parties, such as allies or neighboring states, can help to ensure that promises will be kept, timetables will be respected, and matching commitments will be fulfilled. Third-party tasks may include overseeing and monitoring cease-fires, weapons stockpiles, prisoner releases, and the return of refugees. Having such guarantors in place as part of an implementation plan enhances confidence in the settlement and encourages parties to take the risks that progress toward peace entails.

- **Use external monitors and guarantors to enhance confidence in the settlement.**
- **Develop a network of donors to support implementation.**
- **Use external experts to support implementation.**
- **Engage other communities that have successfully emerged from conflict.**

A network of donors, including governments, aid organizations, and reconstruction agencies, can help pay the bills of implementation. Funds will be needed both for immediate tasks such as cantoning soldiers and transporting refugees and for lengthy reconstruction efforts. Peace will not take root if funding is prematurely terminated. Donors' willingness to coordinate their activities and determination to stay the course are essential to success.

External experts can offer counsel through working groups, commissions, and advisory positions on many aspects of the implementation of a peace accord. They might, for instance, provide guidance on writing a constitution, choosing transitional justice mechanisms, drafting election rules, vetting and training civilian police, conducting a census, and managing natural resources and arranging revenue sharing.

Other communities that have successfully emerged from conflict can share their experiences by participating in formal events and by hosting delegations from (or by dispatching their own delegations to) societies currently struggling to build peace.

Conclusion

Granting that mediation is an art, we hope that we have demonstrated in this handbook that lessons gleaned from the experience of many mediations as set forth in these pages will be helpful and will increase the likelihood that future interational mediation efforts will succeed. Every mediation situation is unique and some of the prescriptions set out here will apply in certain circumstances while others will not, but we believe that the guidelines set out above will be generally instructive both to new and even to experienced mediators.

Acknowledgments

The authors of this handbook and the editors of *The Peacemaker's Toolkit* series, A. Heather Coyne and Nigel Quinney, gratefully acknowledge the valuable contributions and guidance provided by Chester Crocker, Pamela Aall, Guy and Heidi Burgess, and Patricia Thomson; the thoughtful reviews by Paul Hare and Mohamed Sahnoun; and the supportive patience of Marie Marr Jackson.

About the Authors

Amy L. Smith, Ph.D., is a political scientist. As a senior partner in the consulting firm Social Insight, she writes on a variety of international issues, including conflict management, transitional justice, public health, and education issues. Her work generally concerns extracting public policy recommendations from scholarly research. She has conducted research for, taught for, and worked with a variety of advocacy and policy organizations in the United States, Brazil, and Switzerland. Her publications, in addition to several previous monographs for the United States Institute of Peace, include *A Forced Agreement: Press Quiescence to Censorship in Brazil.*

David R. Smock is vice president of the Center for Mediation and Conflict Resolution at the United States Institute of Peace and associate vice president for the Religion and Peacemaking program. He was previously director of the Institute's Grant Program. He is the author or editor of nine earlier books, including *African Conflict Resolution, Interfaith Dialogue and Peacebuilding, Making War and Waging Peace,* and *The Politics of Pluralism.* He lived for many years in Africa and the Middle East while employed by the Ford Foundation. He holds a Ph.D. in social anthropology and African studies from Cornell University.

About the Institute

The United States Institute of Peace is an independent, nonpartisan institution established and funded by Congress. Its goals are to help prevent and resolve violent conflicts, promote post-conflict peacebuilding, and increase conflict-management tools, capacity, and intellectual capital worldwide. The Institute does this by empowering others with knowledge, skills, and resources, as well as by directly engaging in peacebuilding projects around the globe.